Growing up Safe

Safety
in traffic

Illustrated by Sue Wilkinson

SAFETYVILLE

SAFETY SERIES

PUBLISHER	Joseph R. DeVarennes
PUBLICATION DIRECTOR	Kenneth H. Pearson
ADVISORS	Roger Aubin
	Robert Furlonger
EDITORIAL MANAGER	Jocelyn Smyth
EDITORS	Ann Martin
	Robin Rivers
	Mayta Tannenbaum
PRODUCTION MANAGER	Ernest Homewood
PRODUCTION ASSISTANTS	Catherine Gordon
	Kathy Kishimoto
PUBLICATION ADMINSTRATOR	Anna Good

SPECIAL CONSULTANT	*Barbara Jarvis*
ILLUSTRATION AND DESIGN	Sue Wilkinson

Canadian Cataloguing in Publication Data

Main entry under title:

Traffic safety

(Growing up safe)
ISBN 0-7172-2379-5

1. Traffic safety and children—Juvenile literature.
I. Wilkinson, Sue.   II. Series

HE5614.T72 1988   j363.1'2575'088054   C88-093196-5

Come join Jessica, Trevor and Lori Bearberry as they find out everything they need to know about traffic safety.

ALWAYS WALK ACROSS THE ROAD.

ALWAYS HOLD A GROWNUP'S HAND WHEN YOU CROSS THE STREET.

WALK FACING THE TRAFFIC IF THERE IS NO SIDEWALK.

LOOK BOTH WAYS BEFORE YOU CROSS THE ROAD.

NEVER CROSS THE STREET FROM BETWEEN PARKED CARS.

STOP WHEN THE TRAFFIC LIGHT IS YELLOW.

If you are in the middle of the street when the light turns yellow, hurry to the other side.

STOP WHEN THE TRAFFIC LIGHT IS RED.

WALK WHEN THE TRAFFIC LIGHT IS GREEN.

REMEMBER TO LOOK ALL WAYS
EVEN IF THE TRAFFIC LIGHT IS
GREEN.

WAIT TO CROSS THE STREET IF AN EMERGENCY VEHICLE IS COMING.

Ambulances, fire trucks and police cars can go through red traffic lights in an emergency.

ALWAYS WALK YOUR BICYCLE OR TRICYCLE ACROSS THE ROAD.

WHEN THE CROSSING GUARD MOTIONS YOU TO GO, YOU CAN SAFELY CROSS THE STREET.